THE POLITICS OF
SOUTHWESTERN WATER

The
POLITICS
of
SOUTHWESTERN
WATER

by

Ryan J. Barilleaux

COPYRIGHT 1984

TEXAS WESTERN PRESS

The University of Texas at El Paso

ISBN 0-87404-149-X

ABOUT THE AUTHOR

Ryan J. Barrilleaux is a native of southern Louisiana who has been transplanted to Texas. In 1979 he graduated from the University of Louisiana, *summa cum laude*, with a Bachelor of Arts degree in political science. He then did graduate study work at The University of Texas at Austin and received a Master of Arts degree in 1980. He earned his doctorate in government in 1983. Since then he has been an assistant professor of political science at The University of Texas at El Paso. His work has appeared in such journals of scholarship as *American Political Science Review, Presidential Studies Quarterly,* and *Chronicles of Culture.*

Professor Barilleaux dedicates this monograph to his colleagues in the Department of Political Science at The University of Texas at El Paso.

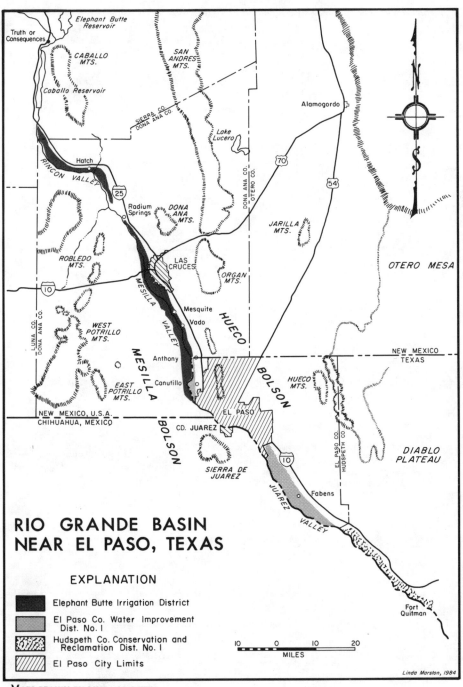

RIO GRANDE BASIN
NEAR EL PASO, TEXAS

EXPLANATION

- Elephant Butte Irrigation District
- El Paso Co. Water Improvement Dist. No. I
- Hudspeth Co. Conservation and Reclamation Dist. No. I
- El Paso City Limits

MAPS DRAWN BY LINDA MARSTEN

Linda Marston, 1984

Preface

The southern United States has come to be widely known as the "Sun Belt," where the warm weather and bright sun have encouraged phenomenal economic growth in recent years. Indeed, this appellation is especially appropriate to the southwestern part of the nation, for it is a desert region with plenty of sun. The rush to leave the "Frost Belt" of the Northeast has had a dramatic effect on the Southwest, creating boom towns of such cities as Los Angeles and Phoenix. Yet there is a more ominous connotation to the growth of the Sun Belt: the Southwest has dwindling water supplies for its growing population.

The Southwest has become the fastest growing region in the nation, causing a shift in the center of the United States population away from the Northeast. But this growth has been dependent on the availability of adequate supplies of clean, fresh water to support agricultural irrigation and the blossoming Sun Belt cities. Not only is the future growth of this region dependent on the continued availability of water, but so is support of the current life of the Southwest.

Yet water supplies in the Southwest are dwindling. Aquifers which supply cities such as Tucson and El Paso are being depleted, the rivers such as the Colorado can only provide limited amounts of water in this rapidly developing region.

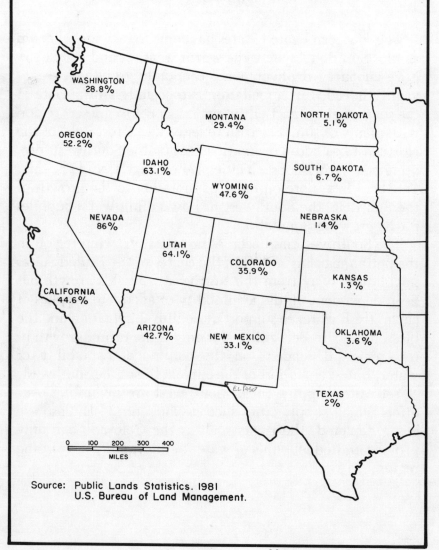

FEDERAL LAND OWNERSHIP
IN THE WEST
(PERCENT OF STATE TERITORY)

WASHINGTON
28.8%

OREGON
52.2%

MONTANA
29.4%

NORTH DAKOTA
5.1%

IDAHO
63.1%

SOUTH DAKOTA
6.7%

WYOMING
47.6%

NEVADA
86%

NEBRASKA
1.4%

UTAH
64.1%

COLORADO
35.9%

CALIFORNIA
44.6%

KANSAS
1.3%

ARIZONA
42.7%

NEW MEXICO
33.1%

OKLAHOMA
3.6%

EL PASO

TEXAS
2%

0   100   200   300   400
MILES

Source: Public Lands Statistics. 1981
U.S. Bureau of Land Management.

MAPS DRAWN BY LINDA MARSTEN

THE POLITICS OF
SOUTHWESTERN WATER

Chapter I
The Water Issue

Water as a Political Issue — The contrast between demand and supply has led to a number of disputes over water, pitting those who have it against those who want it. In Colorado, "have-not" Denver seeks water from the state's less populated areas on the western slope of the Rockies.[1] Likewise, Los Angeles is locked in battle with northern California over diversion of northern water to the arid south.[2] New Mexico is currently fighting an attempt by the West Texas city of El Paso to drill for water in southern New Mexico. Moreover, disputes such as these promise to grow more intense as the high growth rate of the Southwest adds to the burden on already meager supplies.

These modern disputes over water are reminiscent of the rancher-farmer water battles of frontier days, but are quite unlike those earlier contests in an important respect. While earlier water wars were often waged with firearms over private access to water sources, modern water disputes quickly become political battles, pitting different states or parts of

[1]

states against one another in courtrooms and legislative lob-
bies. The result is that water, always extremely valuable in
the Southwest, has become one of the most controversial
political issues in the region.

As such, the water issue raises a number of tough
political questions which must be addressed by government
at all levels. These questions will influence the course of
public policy in the matter of water, and may also affect the
distribution of power in the American federal system. For
as government responds to the water issue and the question
it raises, so policy will be shaped. At the same time, as this
policy development occurs, the role of different governmental levels will be defined: the distribution of power among
states, local governments, and the federal government will
be affected.

These difficult questions confronting government can be
easily stated, even if they are complex in their implications.
There is the fundamental question of what role government
should take in dealing with water problems, but it is a question that is currently being pushed aside as battle lines are
drawn in state legislatures or at state boundaries. Nevertheless, it will continue to be important even when other problems are solved, because it will determine the shape of public water policy. Once jurisdictional disputes are resolved,
the prevailing authority will be faced wth the question of
what role to play in regulating water. Then there is the
question of priorities: should people be favored with water,
or should agriculture? Sun Belt cities such as El Paso, Phoenix and Los Angeles want water for their growing populations, while farmers and ranchers accuse them of waste and
argue that they themselves have a more immediate need.

Perhaps the most pressing question, however, is that of
jurisdiction and control: the issue of who does control and

who should control water resources. This question has come to dominate many of the disputes over water, because it can and will influence the resolution of other issues: water policy, whether in the matter of priorities or the amount of governmental involvement, waits in large part on the answer to the question of who makes policy. This question goes beyond being merely one of who sets policy, but also involves the very distribution of power in the American federal system. For the water issue is increasingly framed in terms of state versus federal control of water resources: states such as New Mexico insist on state control, in order to protect their water from neighbors who want it, while "have-nots" such as El Paso insist on federal limits to the power of "haves" to deny them water. Those who favor state control argue that water resources have always been under state authority, and that these resources must continue to be so controlled in order to protect state interests.[3] Their opponents contend that water crossing state lines is a commodity subject to federal regulation, or that water resources are too important to the nation to be left in the hands of the states.[4] However it is resolved, this question will affect who determines water policy and will thus affect both interstate and intrastate disputes.

The overall issue, then, is what public policy should be as regards water. Should there be a national water policy, even if it favors state controls? If there is one, what form should it take? Who should control water policy? What priorities should be adopted? All of these questions are important and they frame the water issue that is so relevant to the Southwest.

The purpose of this paper is to examine the water issue in the Southwest, with particular attention to its implications for public policy and the distribution of power in the federal system. For water policy has become an important public issue and it will affect the course of American government now and in the future.

In order to accomplish a more instructive examination of these questions, this paper will focus on a significant controversy which is particularly relevant to the larger water issue: the El Paso-New Mexico dispute. This case is a crucial one for understanding the complexities and implications of the Southwestern water issue, because it is in many respects a microcosm of the larger problem. It involves questions of interstate and international dimensions, and illustrates how the water issue can affect the future of federalism. It also demonstrates the clash of priorities which water scarcity engenders. Finally, it illuminates how and where battles over water will be fought. In short, it provides a picture of the water issue in miniature.

Water Policy in the Federal System — The question of the control of water resources has become a crucial one largely because of the federal structure of the American political system. American federalism, particularly in the area of natural resources regulation, is marked by a mixture of national and state governmental authority. Indeed, there is significant overlapping of governmental responsibility for water resources between the two levels.

Historically, states have had extensive discretion in water resource management: controlling supplies, water usage, quality, and distribution. Some states, such as New Mexico and Nebraska, have developed sophisticated systems of water rights laws and institutions to regulate their water resources,[5] while other states, such as Texas, have employed a more fragmented approach to water management. Furthermore, because of the obvious scarcity of water in the arid Southwest, even states with fragmented water management systems have guarded their powers as jealously as comprehensive-control states. Consequently, many states, among them Texas and New Mexico, attempted to prevent any water from leaving their territories.

Yet, while the states have had considerable discretion, the federal government has also been long and deeply involved in water policy. This has occurred in several ways. First, the national government owns an enormous amount of land in the Southwest, and the water on or under it is under federal control.[6] Second, the United States government controls more than 25,000 inland waterways, which include the Mississippi, Ohio, and Columbia rivers.[7] Since 1824, these waterways have been maintained by the Army Corps of Engineers, and they are also policed by the U.S. Coast Guard.[8] Next, and also of great significance, the national government has long been the primary source of funding for the vast array of dams and other water projects spread throughout the nation, and which have been vital to the development of water resources in the Southwest. Dams, for example, create the reservoirs which are important physical manifestations of water policy.

In recent years, federal water project spending has decreased somewhat, but it shows no signs of disappearing. Fiscal constraints have forced the federal government to reduce appropriations in this area and had to press for a state contribution to all projects.[9] Nevertheless, all indications are that the national government will continue to carry most of the financial burden for these projects in the future.

Not only has the federal government been involved in these various physical aspects of water policy, so has it been closely involved in water resource regulation through a host of water-related legislation. The Land Reclamation Act (1902), the Federal Water Power Act (1920) and a variety of other water quality and usage laws all add up to extensive federal involvement in directing water policy. The result of combined federal and state activities is some confusion over the status of water control.

Because of this overlapping, there is no clear answer to the question of who does control water policy. Both federal and state governments can lay claims to that authority, and both have had long histories of such authority. Each has a variety of laws and claims on his side. As to the issue of who should control water, that is a related but slightly different question. For many, particularly those interested in state control of water resources, acknowledge the present overlapping of authority but seek to give states comprehensive control over their water resources.[10] Others emphasize the national scope of water problems, and seek federal coordination through a national water policy.[11] Indeed, one of the states' biggest fears is that a national plan for controlling water resources will mean an effective end to state influence over water policy and a de facto nationalization of water resources.[12]

This sort of debate is typical of those which have taken place throughout the history of American government. In the Constitution, the framers of that document established a system of federalism as a compromise between national and state interests. By mixing governmental authority, they insured a continuous struggle between state interests and the larger national interest. Their intention was to produce public policies that could reconcile these interests when they conflicted. Consequently, many of the debates over public policy in America have been framed in terms of which level of government should exercise predominant control. Significantly, the trend of the twentieth century has been that these debates have been resolved largely in favor of federal control, a fact which serves as an important reason why state control advocates desire clear recognition of state authority: they do not want water policy to join that trend. Accordingly, New Mexico and Nebraska have sought that recognition in court,[13] while the Council of State Governments and National Governors' Association have pressed for national government recognition (from Congress and the Executive) of state primacy in water management.[14]

This position is opposed by those who fear that state primacy will undercut other interests. This group includes "have-nots" such as the City of El Paso, who fear that state primacy will foreclose a reasonable solution to their water problems by allowing states to adopt protectionist water policies. They desire an interstate water market. Also on this side are environmental groups, who fear that state primacy will mean a dilution of water quality standards. Indians oppose state control because they have substantial water rights claims against the federal government, claims which could be impaired by state primacy.

Much rests on the outcome of this debate. If state primacy is established, then New Mexico will be able to prohibit the export of its water, and El Paso will be forced to look for other water sources in Texas. At the same time, intrastate disputes, such as in California and Colorado, will be settled in the state legislature and state courts. On the other hand, if federal limits on state power are upheld, then the interstate shipment of water will be beyond state control, as will several other aspects of federal water policy involvement. Moreover, if federal control of water resources is increased, as in national water planning or even strict enforcement of existing reclamation and related water laws,[15] then the settlement of even intrastate conflicts may involve the federal government. Consequently, public policy will be significantly influenced by the issue of control.

These sorts of issues are what make the El Paso-New Mexico case relevant to the overall water issue. For it is a controversy which contains most of the elements of the larger issue, and its outcome will probably serve to help shape the direction of future water policy. It thus invites a closer examination.

Chapter II
The El Paso-New Mexico Controversy: A Case Study

The dispute between El Paso and the State of New Mexico is particularly relevant to overall water problems in the United States because it is in many respects a microcosm of the larger scene. For the controversy surrounding El Paso's attempt to secure permits for 326 water wells in southern New Mexico, and that state's attempt to frustrate the city's intentions, reflects many elements of national water difficulties: it has both interstate and international dimensions; it pits urban growth against agriculture; it centers on the issue of who controls water and who ought to control it; and, it illuminates the various weapons which the "haves" and "have-nots" may employ in their struggles over water. Moreover, the ultimate outcome of this dispute will probably affect the settlement of other water disputes in the Southwest.

The Controversy Unfolds

The El Paso controversy arises largely from the particular geography of this case. (See map.) Indeed, it is an excellent example of geopolitics at work, as this case study shall demonstrate. The City of El Paso is located in the Rio Grande Basin in a pass (hence the name "El Paso del Norte") between the Franklin and Juarez mountains, along the east

bank of the river. Across the Rio Grande lies Ciudad
Juarez, in the Mexican State of Chihuahua. El Paso not
only borders on Mexico, but also on New Mexico to the west
and north. It lies only a few miles south of Las Cruces, New
Mexico. To the east of El Paso is desert, while along the
river runs a narrow agricultural belt. Northeast of the city
is the enormous military reservation of Fort Bliss, which extends deep into New Mexico. Lying as it does at this junc-
tion of several borders, El Paso is somewhat isolated from
the rest of Texas while close to Mexico and New Mexico. It
is this proximity to New Mexico which induced El Paso to
seek water sources in that state.

Like most of the Southwest, El Paso has always lived on
the edge of water scarcity. Consequently, it has long been
concerned about its water sources. Currently, El Paso's primary source of water (67%) is the Hueco Bolson lying east
of the city, an aquifer that extends into the Fort Bliss military reservation.[16] It also derives a limited amount of water
from the Rio Grande (11%) and wells in the nearby town of
Canutillo, Texas (22%).[17] Water from the Rio Grande is
apportioned according to a 1938 agreement among the
United States, Mexico, Texas, Colorado, and New Mexico,
known as the Rio Grande Compact, the majority of which
goes to the farms in the river basin.[18] The Hueco Bolson and
Canutillo wells are subject to rapid depletion if pumping is
significantly increased above current levels.[19] By the best es-
timates of research conducted for the El Paso Water Utilities Public Service Board, which governs the city's water
system, these existing water sources will be substantially depleted within a century.[20] Moreover, the city's ability to
handle peak summer water demand may be outstripped before the turn of the next century.[21]

Because of the historically precarious nature of its water

supply, El Paso has long pursued policies designed to extend or increase its resources. Although far from austere, the city has pursued a variety of conservation measures since the late nineteenth century: in 1896, El Paso became the second community in the United States to meter water usage; it prohibits water running in the streets; it has carefully maintained and improved its reservoirs; it emphasizes desert landscaping of homes; and, has a conservation oriented plumbing code for new buildings.[22] At the same time, since its creation in 1952, the Public Service Board (PSB) has been interested in expanding the city's sources of water. During the 1950s, new wells were dug at Canutillo, and in the latter part of that decade the PSB fought unsuccessfully to obtain a larger share of Rio Grande water for the city.[23] In order to insure future supplies, some surrounding communities and most unincorporated land up to the New Mexico border were annexed.[24]

Over the years, the PSB has been particularly concerned about finding new sources of water. During the decade of the 1970s, its main course of action involved negotiations for water under land in Valentine, Texas, which lies to the east of El Paso.[25] The possibility of obtaining water from New Mexico, however, was generally excluded from consideration. Like many other Southwestern states, New Mexico prohibited by law the export of its water.[26] Accordingly, El Paso inquired about the possibility of getting around the ban, but did not pursue this course aggressively until 1978.[27]

El Paso began to seriously pursue New Mexican water after the possibility of water from Valentine disintegrated when much of the land in question was bought by an outside party, thus removing it from consideration.[28] Upon learning of this development, the PSB initiated two courses of action intended to expand supplies in the future. First, it

authorized a water recycling plant to reinject water into the
Hueco Bolson; and second, it contacted a water rights law-
yer to explore ways to challenge New Mexico's water embargo law.[29]

In pursuit of water from New Mexico, in 1978 the PSB re-
tained the law firm of Vincent and Elkins to investigate the
New Mexico embargo statute. In 1980, the firm reported
that El Paso's best course would be to challenge the consti-
tutionality of the New Mexico embargo statute: the law,
they argued, created an undue burden on interstate commerce, and it resembled a similar Texas law which the
United States Supreme Court had judged unconstitutional
over a decade before.[30] Moreover, the attorneys were aware
of a memorandum from an assistant attorney general in
New Mexico which also described the embargo statute as
unconstitutional.[31]

Consequently, the PSB inaugurated a campaign to obtain water from New Mexico. It was specifically interested
in drilling for water in the Mesilla Bolson, an aquifer in
southern New Mexico. Most of the water there lies under
federally owned land (Department of Defense), and there
are no plans for its use by the United States or the State of
New Mexico.[32] On September 5, 1980, the PSB thus authorized its attorneys to file suit against New Mexico over the
embargo law.[33]

It is at this point that the battle for New Mexican water
was joined. For the El Paso suit raised the question of who
does and who should control water, with all the issues and
conflicts which that question implies. It is a battle which
pits El Paso against the State of New Mexico, and which has
not yet been resolved.

El Paso's suit seeks to define a limit to the state's power to
govern water resources. New Mexico ground water law rec-

ognizes the control of ground water by landowners, unless the State Engineer declares a closed basin. As the state's chief water regulation officer, the Engineer is empowered to close a water basin if he determines that it is in danger of damage from unregulated pumping.[34] Upon closing a basin, the State Engineer begins regulating it in the interest of preserving the basin and protecting existing water rights holders.

These provisions for regulating the drilling of wells and pumping of water in a closed basin are part of a larger body of laws and institutions by which New Mexico regulates its water resources. Because of its aridity, the state has long been concerned with the disposition of these resources, and has developed a comprehensive water regulatory structure. It was a pioneer in ground water management among American states. Ground water in a closed (or declared) basin is considered public water and subject to appropriation for beneficial use. The State Engineer measures, appropriates and distributes these waters, and he is bound in his management by a set of guidelines designed, *inter alia*, to protect existing water rights. Another aspect of this water regulatory complex is the ban on exported water from the state.[35] Through this structure the state intends optimum use of its scarce resources by its citizens.

Officials in New Mexico regarded the El Paso suit as an attack on the state's carefully constructed water regulatory structure. Within a week of the filing of the suit, the New Mexico State Engineer, S. E. Reynolds, declared the Mesilla Bolson a closed basin.[36] By this means, he prevented any drilling in the Bolson without a permit from him. El Paso then submitted 326 requests for well permits for the Bolson, which the Engineer rejected on the grounds of the contested embargo statute.[37] El Paso then appealed that

decision on the same grounds as its challenge of the embargo, and the matter is still pending the outcome of the
suit. In the meantime, no permits can be approved by the
Engineer, because he is bound to handle requests sequen-
tially: all requests must wait on the El Paso requests. There
are about two thousand requests in sequence after those of
El Paso, about half of which were filed by a New Mexico
farmer-rancher who wants the water for agricultural use.[38]

On January 17, 1983, United States District Judge Howard Bratton of Albuquerque ruled in favor of El Paso, declaring the embargo statute an undue burden on interstate
commerce.[39] He cited most specifically the 1982 U.S. Supreme Court decision in *Sporhase v. Nebraska*, a case similar to this controversy in which the Court struck down a
Nebraska water embargo statute. The Court ruled water an
article of commerce, thus leaving its interstate regulation to
Congress, and declared public ownership of ground water
(as in a New Mexico closed basin) to be a legal fiction. It
also ruled that, failing congressional regulation of interstate
water commerce, states could regulate the interstate commerce of water only under certain conditions: regulation
must serve a legitimate local interest and have only inciden-
tal effects on interstate commerce.[40] Furthermore, Judge
Bratton ruled that the Supreme Court had established in an
earlier case (*H. P. Hood v. DuMond*) that ". . .a state may
discriminate in favor of its citizens only to the extent that
water is essential to human survival."[41] He thus ruled the
embargo statute unconstitutional.

New Mexico immediately appealed Judge Bratton's decision, and the State Legislature enacted a new law to circumvent the ruling. The new statute allows ground water
to be exported from the state if such export is not contrary
to state water conservation practices nor detrimental to the

welfare of the state's citizens.[42] Moreover, the new law directs the State Engineer to treat in-state and out-of-state well permit requests differently: the Engineer must consider alternative water sources available to out-of-state applicants in his permit request deliberations.[43]

The appeals court vacated Judge Bratton's decision and returned the case to him without commenting on its merits. It directed him to undertake "fresh consideration" of the "respective rights and obligations of the parties in light of whatever intervening changes of law and circumstances are relevant."[44] This action gave El Paso a chance to have Judge Bratton rule on the new New Mexico water statute, and the legal battle was resumed. El Paso wants the revised law examined immediately, while New Mexico wants the city to resubmit its well permit requests.[45] The appeals court ruling implies, however, that the case can be tested on the merits of the revised law.

The dispute is far from over, and may go as far as the Supreme Court. It may not even be settled in court, but in Congress: Representative Joe Skeen (D-New Mexico) has introduced legislation in the House of Representatives to settle an issue such as this by guaranteeing state primacy in water resource management,[46] and Senator Pete Domenici (R-New Mexico) has promised a similar bill in the Senate.[47]

Consequently, a battle still rages between El Paso and New Mexico over the water of the Mesilla Bolson.

The Issues

As in the larger water controversy facing the United States, there are two central issues in the El Paso case: the question of priorities and the question of control. The issue of priorities pits urban life against agriculture, and it is ultimately connected with the question of who does and who should control water.

The conflict of priorities arises from El Paso's location among the agriculture of the Rio Grande Basin. While the city's growth has slowed somewhat from its boom in the early 1970s, El Paso is still a fast-growing community with an ever-expanding need for water. This growth puts increased pressure on the city's water sources, and will accelerate their depletion if pumping is accelerated.[48] This fact, joined with the non-availability of water from Valentine and the rigid allocation scheme of water to Rio Grande farms, has led the city to seek water from the Mesilla Bolson.

Yet New Mexicans respond that 326 wells there for El Paso would threaten agriculture in southern New Mexico.[49] They contend that pumping by El Paso would damage the delicate hydrological balance of that area, thus adversely affecting agriculture there.[50] Moreover, they argue that even the permit requests by El Paso are affecting farming, because the El Paso lawsuit has forced a *de facto* moratorium on new drilling permits until the controversy is resolved: New Mexico farmers cannot receive any new permits, a fact which they claim is destroying their livelihood.

El Paso's rejoinder is threefold. First, it argues that pumping in the Mesilla Bolson by the city will not harm agriculture, because the rate of pumping will not deplete the Bolson. Moreover, the city maintains that the discharge of effluent into the Rio Grande puts more water in the river for farmers downriver, which means that farmers upriver (in New Mexico) will be allowed more river water under the Rio Grande Compact.[51] Second, El Paso argues that pumping from the Bolson will be less damaging to agriculture than being forced to find water in Texas: if it must find

water in Texas, the PSB maintains, this will mean con-
demning and appropriating large tracts of farmland along
the Rio Grande in Texas.[52] The PSB thus contends that New
Mexico wants to damage Texas agriculture in order to un-
fairly protect New Mexico.

Finally, El Paso responds that the urban-agricultural
conflict is further tied to the parochial Texas-New Mexico
controversy in that a prohibition against El Paso will not
stop new wells from being drilled in the Bolson. New wells
in the Mesilla Bolson will be drilled — by a New Mexican
farmer-rancher. In sequence behind the El Paso permit requests are requests by a New Mexican agriculturist for
1,034 well permits (over three times the number of the El
Paso requests). According to S. E. Reynolds, the New Mexico State Engineer, there is no way that those requests can
be blocked if El Paso's requests are ultimately denied.[53] In
other words, the water of the Mesilla Bolson will be
pumped; the issue is whether it will be pumped for the benefit of the El Paso urban area or New Mexican agriculture.

The shape of this priorities conflict is the reason it is so
closely tied to the matter of control. For there is not only a
conflict between the city and agriculture, but also one over
whose agriculture will be affected. New Mexico maintains
that it is Texas agriculture which must bear the burden. El
Paso maintains that its danger to New Mexican agriculture
is minimal, and that New Mexico merely wants to penalize
Texas farms through the unfair protection of the New Mexican economy.

The resolution of this conflict turns on the question of
control. If New Mexico's power to control water is upheld,
then it will do so to the benefit of its own farmers. This outcome will most likely also mean an end to most of the Texas
agriculture around El Paso. If the state's power is limited,

then El Paso will be able to obtain the water it needs for its growing population without devastating local farms or, as the city maintains, harming the Mesilla Bolson.

Consequently, as in the larger water issue, the question of control becomes paramount. It pits New Mexico's claim to sovereignty over its water against El Paso's claim that only the federal government can regulate interstate commerce. Moreover, it embodies a dispute over who should control water policy: the states, the national government, or some combination of two powers.

El Paso's argument, which is reflected in its lawsuit against New Mexico, is that a state cannot regulate interstate commerce, so New Mexico cannot discriminate against out-of-state applicants for well permits. The city does not challenge the power of New Mexico to regulate pumping and to protect water resources,[54] only the state's claim to absolute sovereignty over water. The El Paso position, then, is that state power over water extends to regulation for maximum public benefit, but that states should not exercise unlimited control over water: the city wants a mixture of state and federal control over water.

What El Paso seeks in the matter of control over water policy is, to New Mexico, a threat to the state's livelihood. New Mexico maintains that water is and ought to be completely under state control. Yet the "is" part of New Mexico's position is somewhat shaky. Since Judge Bratton declared the New Mexican concept of public water in a closed basin to be a "legal fiction,"[55] the state has explored ways to insure that water in the state is truly public in nature. Most recently, a committee in the New Mexico House of Representatives recommended a study of the feasibility of the state appropriating all unappropriated water in the state.[56] Such a move would effectively "nationalize" all unappropriated water in New Mexico, because the state would now own it, in order to remove any shadow of "legal fiction" from the concept of public water in a closed basin. Such a move would also effectively admit the weakness of the state's claim that it now possesses complete authority over its water.

If the state's claim about who currently controls water is shaky, there is no doubt about whom New Mexico thinks should control it. For the state's public officials, from the Governor, Lieutenant Governor, and State Engineer, to members of Congress, all agree that states should have complete control over their water resources. Not only does the state appear willing to "nationalize" its water in order to gain that control, but members of the state's congressional delegation have introduced bills in Congress to recognize the power of states to control their water.[57] It is clear that the officials of New Mexico want no division of authority between federal and state governments, but only state authority.

In the matter of the two central issues, each side in this dispute has adopted the position which each believes will advance its interests. El Paso wants to see water flow across state lines, while New Mexico believes that state primacy is the best way to protect its interests. The resolution of these issues could affect the future course of American water policy.

Responses to the Controversy

This dispute has engendered a number of responses, ranging from legislation to rhetorical escalation. These responses, as well as the battlegrounds on which the controversy is fought, are important in that they reveal much about coming water controversies in the Southwest.

The first response has been litigation. Of course, El Paso's quest for New Mexican water is being pursued through the lawsuit described above, but it is likely that this suit will not be the only one to arise from the dispute. Jim Ikard, former president of the Las Cruces Chamber of Commerce, is exploring the possibility of a class-action suit against El Paso by "aggrieved" water users in New Mexico.[58] According to Ikard, the *de facto* moratorium on well permits which has resulted from the El Paso lawsuit has restricted economic development in Las Cruces and the rest of southern New Mexico.[59] Such a countersuit would complicate and intensify the controversy over water.

At the same time, legislation is another significant type of response to this dispute. Indeed, activity in this area has been particularly important in that it might shape or alter the outcome of litigation. The first type of legislative response has been in the New Mexico Legislature's attempt to circumvent an outcome adverse to New Mexico's interests. Since Judge Bratton's first decisions in 1983, New Mexican officials have been concerned that the state's water embargo might ultimately be held unconstitutional by the United States Supreme Court. Consequently, the Legislature has made a number of moves to protect state control over water and circumvent such an outcome. As noted above, it enacted a revised water statute which does not absolutely prohibit export but does discriminate between in-state and out-of-state well applicants. In 1984, the Legislature began studying the possibility of "nationalizing" all unappropriated water in the state so that it would indeed be under state control. Finally, the Legislature has approved a proposal to declare a moratorium on new well permits (except for homes and livestock tanks) for two years, and it is likely to become law before the end of 1984[60] This moratorium proposal is designed to further encumber El Paso's attempt to obtain water from the Mesilla Bolson.[61]

While the Legislature attempts to circumvent the possibility of an adverse ruling, members of Congress from the state seek to eliminate the need for a ruling. As noted above, members of New Mexico's delegation to Congress have introduced (or promised to do so) legislation to guarantee states' power to control their own water. Again, the water battle has turned the legislative chamber into a battleground.

Yet there are also other battlegrounds: the mass media and the public forum. Since El Paso began its attempts to obtain water from New Mexico, there has been a hot public debate over the case. This debate, which has been carried on in the congress, at public meetings, and even on automobile bumper stickers, has been marked by rhetorical escalation and the politicization of scientific expertise.

Citizens of El Paso and of New Mexico have each used the public forum to explore their side of the controversy. Water is a hot topic at meetings of civic organizations, Chambers of Commerce, and local government meetings. In Las Cruces, a group called Concerned Citizens For New Mexico Water Resources has organized to present New Mexico's arguments in the controversy to the public.

And the debate has not maintained a moderate tone. The Elephant Butte Irrigation District, a special district governing certain water resources in New Mexico, distributes auto bumper stickers admonishing "Thou shalt not covet thy neighbor's water."[62] Meanwhile, John Salopek, an official of the district, has escalated the verbal war by arguing, "As far as we're concerned, this [El Paso's suit] is nothing less than a well-planned invasion by a *foreign country*, and we'd rather spend our last dollar fighting El Paso than lie down." [Emphasis added.][63]

There has also been talk of an economic boycott of El Paso by New Mexicans, although little has come of it. While it is not widely endorsed by state officials or the Concerned Citizens group, the "Buy New Mexico" campaign has received the highly visible support of the state's Lt. Governor, Mike Runnels.[64] In line with the boycott, Stahmann Farms, a New Mexico pecan grower, has withdrawn its corporate account from an El Paso bank.[65] Yet the boycott has not had a significant impact on El Paso's economy,[66] largely because the economy of southern New Mexico is heavily dependent on business from El Paso.[67]

These battles in public forum have often been waged through the use of scientific experts by each side, each giving his analysis of the scientific evidence in the controversy. The result has been the politicization of scientific expertise, as New Mexico's experts square off against El Paso's experts in the battle to provide scientific justification for each side's position. The problem is that hydrology, like any other science, is inexact, and predictions of what will develop in the future, whether it concerns El Paso's water supply or pumping in the Mesilla Bolson, are based on a combination of evidence and interpretation. Thus science is politicized as differing interpretations of hydrological evidence are offered, and then used as ammunition in the battle over New Mexico water.

The consequence of this development is that the public forum, like the legislative chamber and the courtroom, serves as yet another battleground in the controversy over water. Each side has responded to the dispute in ways that it believes will best advance its cause. The result has been a heightening of tension as the dispute progresses.

The Larger Relevance

This case is relevant to the larger water issue in several respects. First, as a microcosm of the large issue in the Southwest, the El Paso-New Mexico controversy illuminates the central issues which will be debated in other water disputes, the tactics and responses of the parties involved, and the battlegrounds where these disputes will take place. It is clear from this case that everything from litigation to boycott to politicized expertise will be employed to fight coming water battles, and that the parties involved will take their cases wherever they must if they believe it can have an effect on the outcome. Thus, Southwestern water disputes will not be confined to the courtroom, but will enter Congress, state legislatures, and the public forum. The central issue will be that of control, and closely tied to it will be hard questions of future policy priorities. In short, this case is a preview of things to come.

It may also be an important precedent for resolving future disputes over water. First, a Supreme Court decision in this case, which may well be the ultimate result of El Paso's lawsuit, could provide an important precedent for other interstate disputes. If El Paso wins, then the principle of water as an article of interstate commerce could govern the resolution of other controversies: a line would be drawn between federal and state water authority. This result would affect water laws in all Southwestern states. If New Mexico is victorious, then state primacy would be the doctrine governing water resources, and even intrastate battles in

California and Colorado would have to be settled in the
respective state legislatures or courts.

At the same time, this case may provide a precedent in a
second respect: by engendering congressional legislation to
resolve interstate disputes. New Mexico's members of Congress want to resolve this controversy through a law guaranteeing state sovereignty over water. If they are successful
in this campaign, then the El Paso case will neutralize
judicial decisions and direct the outcome in this and future
cases. On the other hand, as Senator Domenici has noted,
there are those in Congress who seek legislation favoring El
Paso's position.[68] If they are successful in this campaign,
then the El Paso case will be the source of important national water legislation which will provide for an even
more active role by the federal government in water regulation.

Another issue of larger relevance is that of federalism, for
this case is intimately bound up with questions of federal-
state relations. Indeed, the legal and legislative decisions set
into motion by this case could well affect the future course
of American federalism.

As noted above, this case involves a fundamental question of whether water is to be treated as an article of interstate commerce, and thus subject only to federal regulation,
or whether water is a vital resource subject to state control.
The answer to this question will affect federalism by defin-
ing the powers of federal and state governments. Historically, states have exercised extensive control over their
water resources, and a resolution of this question in their
favor would put a limit on federal power. It would em-
power New Mexico to resolve this controversy as it chooses.

On the other hand, the federal government has long been
involved with water resource management. Moreover, it

has historically asserted its predominance in governing interstate commerce. The interstate commerce clause of the
United States Constitution has long been interpreted to
mean almost anything resembling commerce between
states, thus broadening federal authority into areas once
considered the purview of states: labor regulation, food
purity, petroleum and mineral resources, exploitation, environmental pollution. The trend of American political
history is that of a broader and broader scope for federal
authority, regardless of state intentions and reservations.
Analogous to water in this regard is the case of petroleum:
states may regulate drilling of wells, well spacing, and the
pumping of oil, because these activities go on in one state,
but they may not regulate the interstate transport of oil.
Texas, despite its disjointed water regulatory structure, has
a centralized agency for petroleum regulation in the
quaintly named Texas Railroad Commission.[69] If water is
established as an article of interstate commerce, then state
regulation of water resources will be restricted to well permits, drilling and pumping regulations, and related activities of intrastate water resource management. There will
be a continued division of federal and state authority.

In a related issue, there is the matter of federal lands in
the Southwest. The United States government owns large
portions of the total land area in Southwestern and Western
states,[70] including 33.1% of Arizona, and 64.1% of Utah.[71]
Indeed, as noted above, most of the land from which El
Paso wants to pump Mesilla Bolson water is federal land,
and the United States government has no objections to El
Paso having the water. On the other hand, the federal
government will not permit the city to drill for water on the
Fort Bliss reservation in Texas, despite the presence of
available water there.[72]

These lands could be important to the resolution of water controversies in that the federal government does not yield to the states on the issue of who controls these lands. They are clearly federal lands, administered through the Bureau of Land Management.[73] If the national government chooses to assert control of the water on or under these lands, then there will probably be little that the states can do to stop it. With this in mind, it is possible to say that the long-term settlement of Southwestern water controversies may well turn on the management and disposition of federal lands in the region.

For the coming water crises in the Southwest are likely to place increasing pressure on the federal government to "do something" about water scarcity. If pressed for water for their growing population, cities such as Los Angeles, Tucson, Phoenix and El Paso will likely turn to the federal government for help. The trend of the twentieth century has been for cities to turn to the national government for help with such problems as urban transit, maintenance of law and order, economic and community development, and education, and to find help there. In the same way, it is probable that Southwestern cities would seek and find help in providing water to their residents. Such help will likely be financial, but may also include water from federal lands in the Southwest.

The El Paso case indicates important ways in which federalism could be affected by the water issue. The powers of the states could be enhanced or they might be diminished, depending on how this issue is resolved. In this way, the El Paso case has a larger relevance in that it may precipitate a move in one direction or the other to resolve the questions raised.

Finally, there is an international dimension to this case

which has relevance to the larger water problems of the Southwest. El Paso shares the Hueco Bolson with Cd. Juarez, Mexico. Juarez gets its water from that bolson and from the Rio Grande (according to the Compact of 1938). Officials in Juarez estimate that the city will not be able to obtain sufficient water from present sources as soon as 1990, and will need additional sources. The prospects are to obtain more water from the Rio Grande and/or to pump water from the Mesilla Bolson, which crosses the Mexico-New Mexico border.[74] Getting more water from the Rio Grande would mean renegotiating the Compact of 1938, but Juarez could pump from the Mesilla Bolson without the permission of New Mexico. Mexico's activities in seeking water for the future will put an additional strain on Southwestern water resources, and it is highly unlikely that Mexico will be a source of water for any part of the Southwest.

As the water issue grows more pressing in this region, it will become increasingly clear how the border can affect the resolution of this issue. For Southwestern cities will not be able to look south for water, and are instead likely to find Mexico a source of competition for water resources. It is beyond the scope of this monograph to examine all the implications of the international dimension to the water issue, except to note that the fact of the border puts a southern limit on possible sources of water.

In summary, it is clear that the El Paso-New Mexico water controversy is a crucial case for understanding the Southwestern water issue and its various complications. Not only is this case something of a microcosm of the larger problem, but it may also provide an important precedent for resolving other disputes over water. Moreover, it may set into motion events and processes which will shape water policy far into the future.

Chapter III
The Uncertain Future

As the El Paso case makes clear, the water issue is far from being resolved. Nevertheless, as a result of this controversy and its implications, the process of resolution may already be beginning. It is likely to be a slow and difficult process and, for nearly all parties involved, a painful one.

Lessons From the El Paso Case

As the case study above demonstrates, the El Paso-New Mexico dispute encompasses most aspects of the larger water problem: the issues, responses of the parties, and the hard choices involved. Consequently, it offers a number of lessons for observers and analysts of that larger issue.

The first lesson regards the sensitivity of the water issue and the lengths to which each party to this controversy will go to press its respective case. As the El Paso case demonstrates, the partisans often look upon the battle for water as something akin to outright war. That is why the controversy has gone beyond the courtroom, entering the legislative chamber and the public forum. That is why talk of an economic boycott is taken seriously, even if such a boycott could be disastrous to the boycotters. That is why rhetorical escalation and the politicization of expertise have occurred.

The water issue is not taken lightly, but as a matter of utmost importance.

The lesson, then, is that all of these responses will be seen more and more often as other battles for water are joined. Moreover, they could make it more difficult to settle various water disputes, because of the heightened emotionalism engendered by the conflict.

Second, as the El Paso case also demonstrates, the resolution of water disputes will involve some hard choices. In that case, there is not only a conflict between agriculture and urban life, but also between the agricultural prosperity of two states. Moreover, there is something of a conflict between state control over water and economy: one reason El Paso is pressing its suit against New Mexico is the dramatically higher cost of alternative water sources.

There are, as El Paso sees it, three major alternatives to New Mexican water. The first, discussed above, would be to condemn and appropriate agricultural land around the city, in order to obtain for the city water currently used for irrigation. Not only would this move damage Texas agriculture in general and the economic health of the El Paso area in particular, but there is also concern about the environmental impact of such a move.[75] Moreover, the amount of water obtained in this way would be insufficient to accommodate the city's long-term water needs. Second, the city might attempt to import water from other parts of Texas. There is water in the Trans-Pecos region about 100 to 150 miles east of El Paso, and also water even further east.[76] Yet intra-Texas importation of water is likely to be very expensive: the Trans-Pecos water would not only be costly to transport; it would also be of limited quantity. Also, its shipment to El Paso would damage agriculture in the Trans-Pecos area. And while water east of the Trans-

Pecos region is in a greater quantity, its shipment over more than 200 miles to El Paso would be even more expensive.[77] Finally, the city might undertake desalinization of salt water in the Hueco Bolson. Yet this solution is expensive in three ways: the cost of a desalting plant is very high, the process itself is energy-intensive, and the cost of disposing of the highly concentrated brines which it produces is an additional expense.[78]

The expense of these alternatives means that New Mexico's control over water competes with economy in water management. If El Paso is denied access to water from the Mesilla Bolson, it will be forced to adopt one or more of these alternatives. Given their expense, the city will probably have to seek financial help from alternative sources. Considering the overwhelming trend of the twentieth century, that help will likely be sought from the federal government.[79] In a time of strain on the federal budget, this fact could present policymakers in the national government with a hard choice between state control over water resources and economy in water resources.

This kind of choice reveals the final lesson of the El Paso case: that there is no easy answer to the question of who does and who should control water. As noted earlier in Part I, water resources are controlled by a confusion of federal and state laws and institutions. Moreover, as this case demonstrates, there are no clear and obvious ways to sort out who should control what because of the trade-offs which water control implies. There are trade-offs between urban and agricultural development, the economies of neighboring states, and state interests and the national interests. With these sorts of complications involved, efforts to resolve the conflicting demands and priorities with a simple, direct solution may not hold up in the long run.

Implications For the Future

Not only does the El Paso case offer a number of lessons regarding the future course of water disputes, but it also contains a number of implications for the future of water policy. These are implications for the future shape of federalism in the matter of water.

First, it is clear that American states will not quietly surrender control over water within their borders. This means that as New Mexico has done, states will attempt to devise a variety of ways to circumvent federally imposed solutions: rewriting embargo laws, declaring moratoria on wells, or employing state capitalism in the control of water. Consequently, it is clear that even a Supreme Court ruling in favor of El Paso may not finally settle the controversy over Mesilla water. For New Mexico will try to undercut the decision, and other states with water embargoes are likely to follow suit.

All of this means that the battle of water is likely to grow more heated as time passes, particularly if New Mexico loses in court. Yet, even if New Mexico is victorious, El Paso's suit has frightened a number of Western and Southwestern states into modifying their water laws to secure state control over water.[80] In short, this means that there will be a protracted controversy over water, no matter the outcome of El Paso's suit against New Mexico.

In spite of this state resistance, and in part because of it, the federal government's role in water policy is likely to grow larger in the future. This is the second implication of the El Paso case. No matter how that case is resolved, or what legislation is passed by Congress in response to the water issue, the federal government's role in water policy will not shrink.

The primary reason for this prediction is the inertia of public policy: the federal government has always been involved in water policy and the twentieth century has seen increasing involvement in that area (land use and environmental legislation). Therefore, as time passes and water scarcity becomes a more pressing issue in the Southwest, federal involvement is likely to grow. If El Paso is victorious in court, then that will mean a federal limit on the power of states to control water. Even if states attempt to circumvent such a ruling through "nationalization" or other means, a Supreme Court judgment of water as an article of commerce will not only limit states but require federal attention to the regulation of interstate water traffic.

At the same time, even a victory for New Mexico, whether in court or in Congress, will not stop the federal government's role from expanding. One case can demonstrate why this is so. California is torn not only by its north-south division, but also by a fight over water in the San Joaquin Valley.[81] The battle pits small farmers and environmentalists against big agribusiness firms over irrigation water. While the intrastate battle does not involve any water except that in California, partisans to the fight have sought and gained federal government action on their behalf: the small farmer-environmentalist side convinced the federal courts to strictly enforce the Reclamation Act of 1902 which sets a limit on the size of farm which may benefit from federally supported irrigation projects.[82] The upshot of this decision has been greater federal involvement without any changes in the law, and in the matter of an intrastate dispute. Considering the complex web of environmental protection and other water-related laws, it is clear that a sanction for state water control would probably not halt growth of the federal role in water policy.

Nor would such a sanction end the demand for federal help in dealing with water problems. As the El Paso case demonstrates, victory for New Mexico could easily mean an increased demand for federal funding of the city's water supply alternatives. Thus a victory for state control would also mean greater federal involvement — and with this greater involvement comes greater control.

For the federal government will be faced with persistent demands for help as Southwestern water scarcity grows more intense, and there is nothing in recent history to suggest that there will be a completely negative response. Rather, it is likely that the federal government will respond favorably to the Sun Belt cities as they demand water for their growing populations (which are also growing in national political power). In responding, the first type of aid will be financial. Yet as water becomes more scarce and long-range transportation schemes grow more costly, the second type of response will be to increase federal control over water resources: the goal will be to protect important population centers, even if doing so tramples on state prerogatives. This sort of response is consistent with federal action in such areas as the environment, education, and urban development. Moreover, with many Northeastern cities (e.g., New York and Boston) desirous of federal aid to help replace their antiquated water systems, there is likely to be a politically powerful coalition of Frost Belt and Sun Belt cities calling for a federal solution to the national problems of water for cities.[83]

In such a climate, the massive amount of federal land in the West will seem to provide a convenient means for beginning to cope with this demand. Without overtly overriding state authority, the national government could easily assert the power to decide what will be done with water on or under United States property, regardless of what a state's laws may be. In the event of that assertion, much of the water in the Mesilla Bolson would be beyond the control of New Mexico. Likewise, other water in the Southwest would be beyond state control. Just as New Mexico can contemplate "nationalization" of water within its boundaries, so the United States government might decide to "nationalize" water on its land.

In summary, then, the major implications of the El Paso case are state recalcitrance in the matter of water control and increasing federal involvement with this issue. Yet growing federal involvement does not necessarily mean an end to any state authority in water policy, as the next section shall indicate.

Possible Scenarios For the Future

As the preceding section has indicated, greater federal control of water is a distinct possibility in the future. Likewise, state interest in retaining control of water is also a clear implication of the El Paso case and other trends. The issue which results from these conflicting extrapolations is what course water policy might ultimately take, and whether there is an inevitability to the prospect of "federalized" water. Examining possible scenarios of future events could suggest some answers.

Scenario 1. Whether by court decision or an act of Congress, state primacy in water control is guaranteed. In consequence, El Paso must seek water elsewhere in Texas, and Western states confirm their water embargo laws. In order to obtain water from expensive alternative sources, El Paso seeks federal help. It is joined in this effort by other

Southwestern cities, such as Los Angeles and Tucson, who are also in need of water, and by Eastern cities requiring renovation of their water facilities.

The federal government responds with financial help, and the bill for water soon becomes staggering. Soon, states such as New Mexico find that they are faced with significantly higher federal taxes, which are required in order to pay for the thirsty cities. As the demand grows more pressing, and costs mount, the federal government attempts to lower costs by using water from federal lands for the cities, such as using the Mesilla Bolson for El Paso. Because New Mexico and other "haves" attempt to establish barriers to the action, as they did to other actions, the national government ignores or even mandates abolition of any state restrictions on water on federal land or intended for interstate transport. The ultimate outcome is the reverse of what the states wanted: a *de facto* nationalization of much Southwestern water and an attendant dimunition of state power.

Scenario 2.   El Paso wins in court and Congress does not mandate state primacy, but states such as New Mexico develop various means to circumvent the decision (e.g., state appropriation of water). The result is similar to that in the first scenario: pressure for federal aid from the cities, clashes between cities and states over water, and eventually a confrontation between states and the federal government. In consequence, the federal government declares water a national resource and assumes complete regulation of it. As in Scenario 1, the ultimate outcome is contrary to what the states thought they would receive.

Scenario 3.   As New Mexico has already begun to suspect, El Paso wins in court. The Supreme Court rules that, while states may regulate drilling and pumping of water in order to protect water resources, only Congress may regulate interstate commerce. Therefore, a state may discriminate against out-of-state well applicants. The result is that an interstate water "market" will develop to complement the intrastate markets already in existence: cities such as El Paso will obtain water from wherever they can, providing they can meet local requirements and pay whatever price is necessary. At the same time, states such as New Mexico will be able to protect the delicate hydrological balances in their territories. When cities call for federal aid for water, such aid will be financial rather than an assertion of authority: there will be no need for bitter fights over state barriers nor the use of overwhelming power to defeat them. Moreover, since there will be less need for long-distance water transit, as in El Paso's expensive alternatives, the cost to all will be lower. The ultimate outcome will be a continued division/overlapping of federal and state authority (depending on how one looks at it), but much less of a threat to state power.

These three scenarios represent a range of likely developments in the water issue, based on the probable courses of action on the part of state and federal governments. As the El Paso case has demonstrated, and as the analysis in Chapter I outlined, two important facts have been extensive state control of water resources, which are jealously guarded, and federal involvement in water policy, which is likely not only to continue but also to respond to the demands for help from the Sun Belt cities. Consequently, it is possible to construct those scenarios and the outcomes to which they might lead.

Conclusions

As this study has shown, the issue of water is not only significant to the future development of the Southwest, but may have significant effects on the future of American federalism. It is clear that water supplies are diminishing in the region, and that this fact directly conflicts with the growth of the Southwest. Accordingly, there are some tough battles over water underway, as the El Paso-New Mexico controversy has shown, as well as more to come in the future.

The El Paso case is thus important not only as a microcosm through which the water issue may be examined, but also because of what it implies for the future of federalism and of water policy. With the pressing need for water in cities such as El Paso, Southwestern states such as New Mexico are probably subverting their long-term interests by attempting to assert absolute sovereignty over their water. Such a course will probably result in undermining federalism as water policy is brought under increasing national control.

As for the future of water policy, it rests on developments in the matter of control. If states do not continue to press for absolute water sovereignty, then they will be able to use their power over drilling to protect their water resources for the benefit of their citizens and state interests. On the other hand, if, as this analysis suggests, the states force a confrontation with a coalition of cities (demanding federal help), then water policy may be redirected toward the benefit of urban centers. States would thus be the losers, and there is a strong chance that Southwestern agriculture might suffer.

For example: if some nationalized water planning were implemented, agriculture in the arid Southwest might be considered a luxury when wetter regions can produce enormous amounts of food.

In the end, then, these questions turn on the question of control. How that question is resolved can determine not only the future course of water policy, but also the future state of American federalism.

APPENDIX

War of Words Over Water

The rhetorical escalation which has marked the public debate over the El Paso-New Mexico dispute illustrates the importance of the water issue in the Southwest. For water is the essential resource of Southwestern life and control over it has always been a primary concern for residents of this region. Consequently, the battles in courtrooms and legislative sessions have been accompanied by a war of words over water.

This war of words can best be seen in the local press of El Paso and New Mexico. The Albuquerque *Journal* and Las Cruces *Sun-News* have vehemently denounced El Paso's efforts to obtain water from New Mexico, Judge Bratton's decision, and any attempts to undercut state primacy in control of water. In contrast, the El Paso *Times* and *Herald-Post* have tended to stress the scarcity of water in the El Paso area and the interdependence of the El Paso-southern New Mexico region.

Typical of El Paso's approach are articles in the *Times* such as "El Paso's Water Well Will Go Dry Someday, So Let's . . . Conserve,"[84] "El Paso Prepares Water Options in Case It Loses Suit,"[85] and "Boycott or Not, New Mexico Counts on Texans."[86] These have been accompanied by editorials stressing interdependence and the need for interstate and international cooperation in solving Southwestern water problems. An essay by Douglas M. Wrenn, an associate of the Urban Land Institute, proclaimed that "Water Will Be to the 1980s What Oil Was to the 1970s:"[87]

Given the urgent need to manage water supplies more effectively, it seems more appropriate for the federal government to coordinate a unified water policy than to allow institutions responsible to different congressional committees to act individually. Each state could also improve the allocation of water by making the laws governing water use uniform across the state and by trying to eliminate the tremendous divergence of state laws.

Independent of whatever changes are made in the water allocation process, it is certain that the magnitude of future water supply problems will depend on how well the nation conserves existing resources. Historically, water has been relatively inexpensive and thus the motivation to save it is not strong. That will change in the future and as the cost of water rises, water users will have to formulate ways to use the resource more efficiently.

Another editorial, by Professor Oscar J. Martinez of The University of Texas at El Paso, focuses on the close links between the components of the El Paso-Las Cruces-Ciudad Juarez area:[88]

The true culprit in the water fight is the irrational boundary drawn more than a century ago. Over the years, many El Pasoans have expressed displeasure over what they feel has been less than equal treatment at the hands of Austin. Often the wish has been heard that El Paso withdraw from Texas and join New Mexico. It may surprise New

Mexicans that attitudes expressed in the Land of
Enchantment toward the Lone Star State are
sometimes found in El Paso as well.

But the legal reality remains. The international
boundary and the state boundary arbitrarily bi-
sect the natural, geographic, economic and cultural entity that is the El Paso-Ciudad Juarez-Las
Cruces metropolitan area.

In the past, these intensely interdependent communities have worked together for the common
good. At times, they have devised effective means
of dealing with border barriers, even ignoring
them when their effect has been detrimental to
mutual well-being. It will be interesting indeed to
see how flexible each side will be in the latest
courthouse maneuverings over water rights.

On the other side of this controversy, the New Mexico
press has presented that state's case against the El Paso
claim for water. In their editorials and news features, the
New Mexico newspapers have stressed their state's aridity
and need for water, the importance of state control over
water resources, and the greed of El Paso.

One of the most outspoken opponents of El Paso's water
quest, who has received significant attention from the Albuquerque and Las Cruces papers, is John Salopek. As a
farmer and president of the Elephant Butte Irrigation District, he has been an unofficial spokesman for the New Mexican position.[89] He characterizes the El Paso suit as "high-
way robbery"[90] and predicts that a victory for El Paso will
result in "the damndest drilling program you've ever
seen."[91] After Judge Bratton's decision in January 1983, the

Albuquerque *Journal* turned to Salopek for an expression of
how the people of New Mexico feel about the El Paso suit:[92]

> "That water is our property," Salopek said bit-
> terly. "This is the most blatant violation of other
> people's rightful property."

> In Salopek's view, the court battle over the wat-
> er is an act of war. "El Paso wants to keep us like a
> colony," he said. "We're a poor state, let's face it,
> and they want to keep us that way."

Likewise, editorials in the *Journal* and *Sun-News* have
denounced El Paso's effort to obtain New Mexican water.
When the suit was filed in 1980, the *Journal* asked "Can
Texans Drain Us?:"[93]

> There can be little challenge to El Paso's
> asserted need for additional water, and there is lit-
> tle doubt that the most convenient unappropri-
> ated sources are in southern New Mexico. El Paso
> points to its continual growth, its prospects for
> further growth and the demands fostered by in-
> dustrialization already set in motion.

> But the same can be said for the New Mexico
> communities lying astride the lower Rio Grande
> and Tularosa basins. Few areas in the nation have
> exhibited more dramatic and consistent growth in
> the era launched by World War II, and the over-
> flow from metropolitan El Paso has been a sub-
> stantial source of that growth.

> Considering the emotional issues, El Paso's
> greed — or thirst — for New Mexico water may
> prove short-sighted and self-defeating. White

Sands Missile Range, which draws its water from the Tularosa Basin, is not only one of the principal employers of El Pasoans, but it also is one of the principal consumers of goods and services generated by the El Paso commercial community.

Furthermore, the traditional loyalties of the thriving communities of southern New Mexico to El Paso as their trade and cultural center would be sorely tested by the water grab. Their own growth potential would be severely impeded by the loss of a vital water source. It is doubtful that the cordial relationships that have been more than a century in the building could survive the predictable resentment.

This essay contrasted New Mexico's need against El Paso's, while other arguments advanced in New Mexico newspapers contrasted that state's prudent use of water resources with El Paso's "greed" and "overuse:"[94]

El Paso had the problem and succeeded in making New Mexico's scarce and diminishing water resources the solution. That in turn has given New Mexico an even bigger problem — protecting its ability to govern its own resources.

Quite simply, New Mexico's border has been breached. Theoretically, outside municipalities or states — or anybody — can now apply to claim every unappropriated drop of New Mexico water. It is ironic because New Mexico has carefully guarded and conserved its water resources, only to lose a lawsuit to a city and state that take far less care of the resource.

U.S. District Judge Howard Bratton threw out
a 1953 New Mexico law prohibiting the exporta-
tion of ground water to other states. The judge, by
ruling that law unconstitutional, cleared the way
for the city of El Paso to buy underground New
Mexico water. The result could harm the ability of
southern New Mexicans to maintain their busines-
ses and farms.

Sen. Pete Domenici, R-N.M., and Rep. Manuel
Lujan, R-N.M., both have said they will propose
legislation to help New Mexico protect its resources. Presumably this means they would attempt to write a federal law giving states the right
to enforce laws similar to the 1953 New Mexico
law Bratton has ruled unconstitutional. Such a
law would be desirable for water-scarce states.
But politically it may be difficult to pass because
those who have overused their share will want to
retain the right to go after another state's water
(El Paso is a good example). And anyway, a new
law would have to meet many conditions before it
could be applied to the El Paso case.

But the *Sun-News* went further than this prudence-over-
use contrast, to proclaim that all that really matters is protecting New Mexico's water for New Mexicans:[95]

If keeping New Mexico water for New Mexico
needs is discrimination, c'est la vie.

The legal rhetoric goes on and on. We fully ex-
pect the debate in appeals to go on and on.

Meantime, aside from any legal wrangle, right
is right and Bratton's findings don't hold water.

Farmer John Salopek probably said it best for all of us: "I don't care, farmers don't care, nobody cares what the judge says. We just don't agree with that ruling. And we will continue our fight."

So, the water controversy, by touching on the sensitive matter of control over a vital resource, has been escalated rhetorically to a war of bitter words and a growing gulf between the opposing sides. Rhetorical escalation is a symptom of this controversy, but it is also more than that: by portraying the dispute as an all-out war, such escalation makes it more and more likely that the water issue in the Southwest will ultimately be settled by confrontation rather than reason.

NOTES

1 "War Over Water," *U.S. News and World Report*, Oct. 31, 1983, p. 59.

2 Ibid.

3 See, for example, "Getting Control of Water," El Paso *Times*, January 1, 1984, p. 10-B; Leonard U. Wilson, *State Water Policy Issues* (Lexington, KY: The Council of State Governments, 1978), p. 5; and, "West Watches Water Battle, Roots For New Mexico," El Paso *Times*, January 4, 1982, p. 1-A.

4 "War Over Water," p. 58; *The City of El Paso v. Reynolds*, Mem. Op., U.S. District Court For the District of New Mexico (1983). (Henceforth: *El Paso v. Reynolds*.)

5 *El Paso v. Reynolds*.

6 Richard D. Lamm and Michael McCarthy, *The Angry West* (Boston: Houghton Mifflin Co., 1982), pp. 235-237. Federal lands amount to large portions of Southwestern states:

New Mexico	33.1%
Arizona	42.7%
Colorado	35.9%
Utah	64.1%
Nevada	86.0%
California	44.6%

7 T. R. Reid, *Congressional Odyssey* (San Francisco: W. H. Freeman and Company, 1980), pp. xii and 4.

8 Ibid.

9 Terry L. Anderson, *Water Crisis: Ending the Policy Drought* (Baltimore: Johns Hopkins University Press, 1983), pp. 112-113.

10 "Congress Interested in Water Tug of War," El Paso *Times*, Dec. 8, 1983, p. 1; H.R. 1207, 98th Cong., 1st sess. (1983); and Lamm and McCarthy, *op cit.*

11 Wilson, pp. 4-5; Douglas M. Wrenn, "Water Will Be to the 1980s What Oil Was to the 1970s," El Paso *Times*, August 21, 1983, p. 2-F.

12 See, for example, Wilson, pp. 5 and 53.

13 *City of El Paso v. Reynolds*.

14 Wilson, pp. 4-12.

15 Current federal water laws provide the potential for greater federal control without national water planning policy. The Land Reclamation Act limits the size of farms, and water quality laws provide a means for controlling what happens to water. Moreover, much land in the Southwest belongs to the federal government, and in the absence of state primacy, might escape state authority.

16 The term "bolson" is from the Spanish word for purse, and is applied in this region to many aquifers, i.e., underground "purses" of water. See Christopher Wallace, *Water Out of the Desert*, Southwestern Studies, Monograph Number 22 (El Paso: Texas Western Press, 1969), p. 6.

17 For detailed statistics on El Paso's water supply, see Lee Wilson and Associates, Inc., *Water Supply Alternatives for El Paso* (El Paso: El Paso Water Utilities Public Service Board, 1981). Percentages cited here are derived from a table on page A-9.

18 Ibid. See also S. E. Reynolds, "The Rio Grande Compact," *International Water Law Along the Mexican-American Border*, ed. by Clark S. Knowlton, Symposium No. 11 of the Committee on Desert and Arid Zones Research, Southwestern and Rocky Mountain Division of the American Association for the Advancement of Science (El Paso: The University of Texas at El Paso and the Committee on Desert and Arid Zones Research, 1968).

19 Wilson and Associates, pp. B-13-B-15.

20 Op. Cit., pp. A-8-A-11.

21 Loc. cit.

22 "El Pasoans Thought Ahead About Water," El Paso *Times*, Oct. 2, 1983, p. 12-E.

23 Wallace, pp. 28-30; "Water Is a Fightin' Word Out West," El Paso *Times*, August 2, 1983, p. 13-A.

24 Wallace, pp. 31-34.

25 Interview with John Hickerson, General Manager, El Paso Water Utilities Public Service Board, El Paso, Texas, November 10, 1983.

26 "EP Water Fight Ripples Across West," El Paso *Times*, August 22, 1983, p. 1. New Mexico, Nebraska, Colorado, Nevada, Montana, Wyoming, Utah, and Texas all recently had or still have some type of water export ban.

27 Hickerson interview.

28 Ibid.

29 Ibid.

30 *City of Altus v. Carr*, 255 F. Supp. 828(W.D. Tex.), *aff'd. mem.*, 385 U.S. 35(1966).

31 Ibid.

32 Ibid.

33 Ibid. To remove all questions of legal standing regarding the suits, the suit was filed in the name of the City and individual members of the PSB as citizens. Moreover, the City Council specifically affirmed the power of the PSB to sue.

34 Ibid. Texas has a similar law, but voters may approve a Water Conservation District in substitute. In general, Texas has much less centralized control of water resources than does New Mexico.

35 *El Paso v. Reynolds.*

36 Hickerson interview.

37 Ibid.

38 Ibid.

39 *Sporhase v. Nebraska*, ____U.S.____, 102 S.Ct.3456 (1982).

40 *El Paso v. Reynolds.*

41 Ibid.

42 1983 N.M. Laws 2.

43 Hickerson interview.

44 Order and Judgment, 10th Circuit Court of Appeals, December 16, 1983, *City of El Paso v. Reynolds*, No. 83-1350.

45 Ibid.

46 H.R. 1207 (see note 10).

47 "Congress Interested in Water Tug of War," *loc. cit.*

48 See II-A above, and sources cited in notes 16, 17, and 18.

49 "Water Worries Worse For Farms Than Industry," El Paso *Times*, August 21, 1983, p. 12-A; and Dr. Leo Eisel, Wright Water Engineers, Inc., public lecture in Las Cruces, NM, October 12, 1983.

50 Ibid. (Both sources.)

51 Hickerson interview.

52 Ibid.

53 Ibid.

54 Plaintiff's Memorandum, *City of El Paso vs. Reynolds*, No. 80-730HB(D.N.M. 1983).

55 See discussion above, and *El Paso v. Reynolds, op. cit.*

56 *"Panel Backs Water Study Appropriation,"* El Paso *Times*, January 31, 1984, p. 3-B.

57 See note 10 above.

58 "Las Cruces Man Wants to Sue El Paso," El Paso *Times*, January 27, 1984, p. 1.

59 Ibid.

60 Ibid., p. 1; "House Approves Well Moratorium," El Paso *Times*, February 4, 1984, p. 4-B; "Committee to Dilute Water Moratorium," El Paso *Times*, Feb. 1, 1984, p. 4-B; "Bill Imposes New Water Well Moratorium," El Paso *Times*, Feb. 15, 1984, p. 3-B.

61 Ibid. (All three sources.)

62 "Water is a Fightin' Word Out West," p 13-A.

63 "War Over Water," p. 59.

64 "New Mexico Dishes Out Watered-Down Boycott," El Paso *Times*, August 21, 1983, p. 1.

65 Ibid.

66 Ibid., p. 12-A.

67 "Boycott or Not, New Mexico Counts on Texans," El Paso *Times*, August 21, 1983, p. 12-A.

68 "Congress Interested in Water Tug of War," *loc. cit.*

69 For a discussion of this area, see David Prindle, *Petroleum Politics and the Texas Railroad Commission* (Austin: University of Texas Press, 1982).

70 For details, see note 6 above.

71 *Loc. cit.*

72 Hickerson interview.

73 See Lamm and McCarthy, Ch. 8.

74 "El Paso, Juarez Told to Share Water," El Paso *Times*, November 16, 1983, p. 1-B.

75 See Wilson and Associates, pp. B-12-B-13.

76 Ibid., pp. B-21-B-22.

77 *Loc. cit.*

78 *Loc. cit.*

79 The federal government has already displayed some interest in helping to fund a solution to water problems in this region. See Wilson and Associates, p. B-25.

80 See "El Paso Water Fight Sends Ripples Across West," *loc. cit.*

81 "War Over Water," p. 58.

82 *Loc. cit.*

83 See *loc. cit.* and pp. 60-62.

84 El Paso *Times*, October 2, 1983, p. 1-E.

85 El Paso *Times*, January 6, 1982, p. 1-A.

86 El Paso *Times*, August 21, 1983, p. 12-A.

87 El Paso *Times*, August 21, 1983, p. 2-F.

88 "Water: Latest Controversy is But One of Many," El Paso *Times*, October 30, 1983, p. 2-F.

89 The Las Cruces *Sun-News* essentially described him as such. See the January 18, 1983 issue, p. 4.

90 "El Pasoans Feel N.M. Water Necessary For City's Future," Albuquerque *Journal*, February 6, 1983, p. B-4.

91 Ibid.

92 "Hard Feelings Persist Over El Paso's Plans," Albuquerque *Journal*, February 6, 1983, p. B-1.

93 Albuquerque *Journal*, September 19, 1980, p. A-4.

94 "State's Border Breached," Albuquerque *Journal*, January 21, 1983, p. A-4.

95 "Here's Mud in Our Eyes," Las Cruces *Sun-News*, Janaury 18, 1983, p. 4.

EDITORIALS QUOTED IN APPENDIX

1 El Paso *Times*
Oscar J. Martinez, "Water: Latest Controversy is But One of Many," October 30, 1983, p. 2-F.

Douglas M. Wrenn, "Water Will Be to the 1980s What Oil Was to the 1970s," August 21, 1983, p. 2-F.

2 Albuquerque *Journal*
"Can Texans Drain Us?," September 6, 1980, p. A-4.

"State's Border Breached," January 21, 1983, p. A-4.

3 Las Cruces *Sun-News*
"Here's Mud in Our Eyes," January 18, 1983, p. 4.

Texas Western Press

gratefully acknowledges
the following endowments:

The Mary Hanner Redford Memorial Fund
The Judge and Mrs. Robert E. Cunningham Fund
The Dr. C.L. Sonnichsen Southwestern Publication Fund

all of which make possible
this and other issues of

Southwestern Studies